# ENGINEERING MARVELS
# KINGDA KA
# ROLLER COASTER

by Vanessa Black

pogo

# Ideas for Parents and Teachers

Pogo Books let children practice reading informational text while introducing them to nonfiction features such as headings, labels, sidebars, maps, and diagrams, as well as a table of contents, glossary, and index.

Carefully leveled text with a strong photo match offers early fluent readers the support they need to succeed.

## Before Reading

- "Walk" through the book and point out the various nonfiction features. Ask the student what purpose each feature serves.
- Look at the glossary together. Read and discuss the words.

## Read the Book

- Have the child read the book independently.
- Invite him or her to list questions that arise from reading.

## After Reading

- Discuss the child's questions. Talk about how he or she might find answers to those questions.
- Prompt the child to think more. Ask: Have you ever ridden on a roller coaster? Would you like to ride the Kingda Ka?

Pogo Books are published by Jump!
5357 Penn Avenue South
Minneapolis, MN 55419
www.jumplibrary.com

Library of Congress Cataloging-in-Publication Data

Names: Black, Vanessa, 1973- author.
Title: Kingda Ka roller coaster / by Vanessa Black.
Description: Minneapolis, MN: Jump!, Inc., [2017]
Series: Engineering marvels | Audience: Ages 7-10.
Includes bibliographical references and index.
Identifiers: LCCN 2017004844 (print)
LCCN 2017005782 (ebook)
ISBN 9781620317020 (hard cover: alk. paper)
ISBN 9781624965791 (e-book)
Subjects: LCSH: Roller coasters—Juvenile literature.
Roller coasters—New Jersey—Juvenile literature.
Amusement rides—New Jersey—Juvenile literature.
Six Flags Great Adventure (N.J.)—Juvenile literature.
Classification: LCC GV1860.R64 B53 2017 (print)
LCC GV1860.R64 (ebook) | DDC 791.06—dc23
LC record available at https://lccn.loc.gov/2017004844

Editor: Kirsten Chang
Book Designer: Molly Ballanger
Photo Researchers: Molly Ballanger & Kirsten Chang

Photo Credits: Noah K. Murray/Star Ledger, cover; New York Daily News Archive/Getty, 1; Adam Ahmed/Flickr, 3, 11; Knut Hildebrandt/imageBROKER/SuperStock, 4; Kotsovolos Panagiotis/Shutterstock, 5; STAN HONDA/Staff/Getty, 6-7, 10; The Star Ledger/Noah K. Murray/The Image Works, 8-9, 20-21; FabrikaSimf/Shutterstock, 12-13; The Star Ledger/Ed Murray/The Image Works, 14-15, 16-17; Brian Branch-Price/AP Images, 18-19; Tim Larsen/AP Images, 23.

Printed in the United States of America at Corporate Graphics in North Mankato, Minnesota.

# TABLE OF CONTENTS

# CHAPTER 1

# BIG THRILLS

You love roller coasters.
You love the speed.
You love the thrill.

Do you want to ride the tallest roller coaster in the world? It is at Six Flags theme park in New Jersey. It is 45 stories high. That is about as tall as 50 elephants standing on top of each other! What is this engineering marvel? Kingda Ka!

Hop in! Get ready for the ride of your life. You will not slowly click up a big hill like you do on some coasters. This is a rocket coaster.

Hang on! You go from zero to 128 miles (206 kilometers) per hour in 3.5 seconds!

**DID YOU KNOW?**

You have to be 4 feet, 6 inches (1.4 meters) tall to ride Kingda Ka. This rule is to keep you safe.

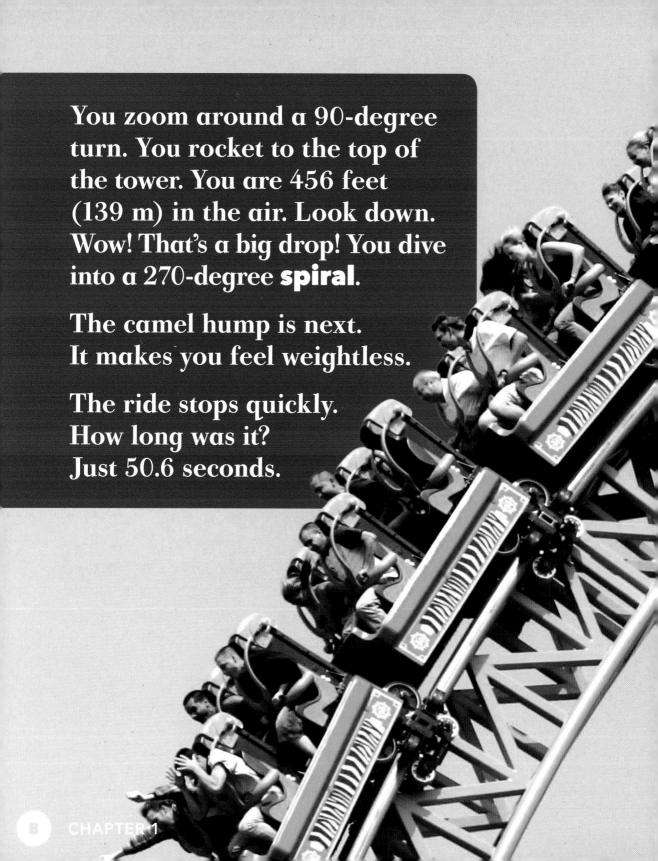

You zoom around a 90-degree turn. You rocket to the top of the tower. You are 456 feet (139 m) in the air. Look down. Wow! That's a big drop! You dive into a 270-degree **spiral**.

The camel hump is next. It makes you feel weightless.

The ride stops quickly. How long was it? Just 50.6 seconds.

# TAKE A LOOK!

What are the parts of the
Kingda Ka roller coaster?

**❶ station**
**❷ tower**
**❸ camel hump**
**❹ train**

# CHAPTER 2
# HOW DOES IT WORK?

When Kingda Ka opened in 2005, it was the tallest, fastest roller coaster in the world.

catch car

How does it work? The train is launched
to high speed by a **hydraulic** system.
At the station, the train is locked onto
the "catch car." It is below the train,
between the two rails of the track.
It is pulled by a **cable**.

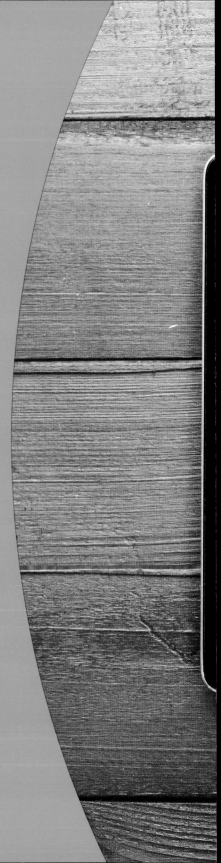

When an operator pushes the launch button, hydraulic pumps fluid push through big motors. This creates **energy**. The energy is stored in **accumulators**. At just the right time, the energy is let go.

The motors spin a **drum**. The drum winds the cable. The cable pulls the catch car down the track. The catch car tows the train rapidly. It releases it just in time, sending the train down the track and up the tower.

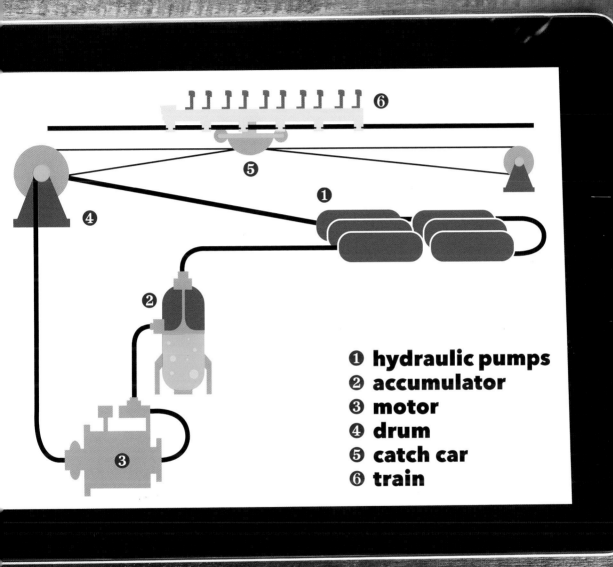

① **hydraulic pumps**
② **accumulator**
③ **motor**
④ **drum**
⑤ **catch car**
⑥ **train**

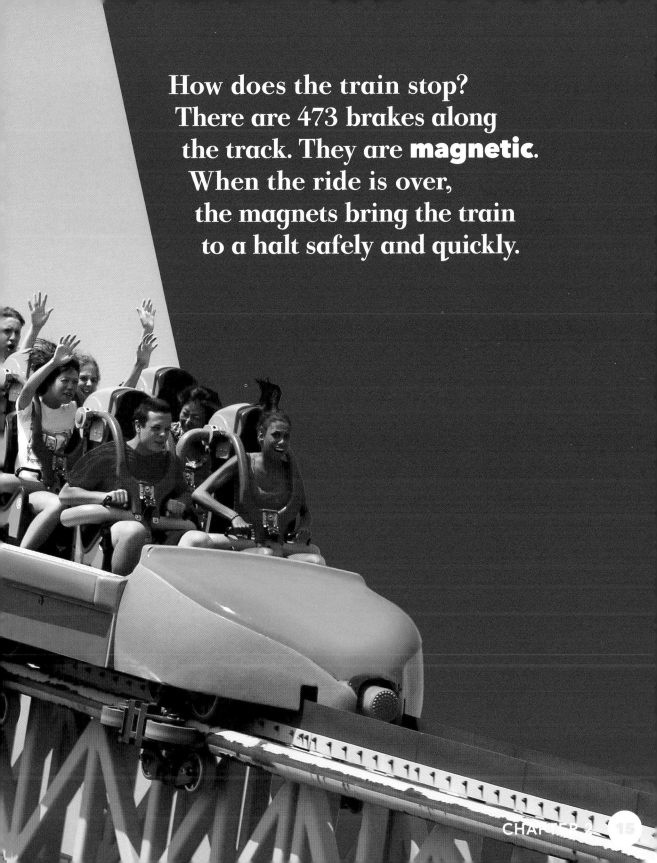

How does the train stop?
There are 473 brakes along
the track. They are **magnetic**.
When the ride is over,
the magnets bring the train
to a halt safely and quickly.

Very rarely, the train doesn't make it over the hill. This can be due to the wind or the weather. **Engineers** plan for this. It is perfectly safe. The train rolls back down the track. Then the riders get launched again!

## DID YOU KNOW?

A single launch tops 12,500 **horsepower**. That's more than 12 times the horsepower of a Formula One race car.

# CHAPTER 3
# CONSTRUCTION CHALLENGES

Workers ran into problems during construction. In 2005, record amounts of snow, high winds, and fog hit New Jersey. The thick fog made it hard for crane operators to see where to put the track.

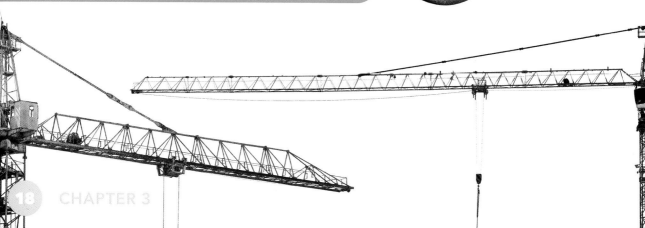

They couldn't work if the winds were too high. They were **delayed** time after time.

Finally, the work was done. It was time to test it. Workers put an empty train on the track. They pushed the launch button. The train shot forward. It climbed the tower. But it didn't make it to the top. It fell back down.

Engineers adjusted the hydraulic system. They tried again and again.

Finally, after 600 hours of test runs, the train made it to the top of the tower. The rest is roller coaster history!

# ACTIVITIES & TOOLS

## UNDERSTAND HYDRAULICS

**How are hydraulics like a water gun? Find out with this activity.**

**What You Need:**

- small squirt gun
- large squirt gun–
  a super soaker type
- water

❶ **Fill the squirt guns with water.**

❷ **Squirt the small squirt gun.**

❸ **Squirt the large squirt gun.**

❹ **Which one has more power? The larger squirt gun. A larger amount of fluid is pushed through a smaller hole, giving the water gun more power. A super soaker is similar to the way the hydraulics work on a rocket coaster.**

**accumulators:** Large tanks that store hydraulic energy.

**cable:** A strong rope made of wires that are twisted together.

**delayed:** Happening later than it should.

**drum:** A large container.

**energy:** Power that is used to operate machines.

**engineers:** People who use science and math to create things that humans use.

**horsepower:** A unit of measurement that describes the rate at which an engine can do work.

**hydraulic:** Moved or operated by the pressure of water or other liquid.

**magnetic:** Having the power of a magnet, which is a piece of iron or steel that can stick to metal.

**spiral:** A curving, circular line that goes around a central point.

# INDEX

# TO LEARN MORE

Learning more is as easy as 1, 2, 3.

1) Go to www.factsurfer.com

2) Enter "KingdaKaRollerCoaster" into the search box.

3) Click the "Surf" button to see a list of websites.

With factsurfer, finding more information is just a click away.